CITY WORKS DEPT.

Philip Hancock was born in Newchapel, Stoke-on-Trent, in 1966. He left school at sixteen to serve a City & Guilds craft apprenticeship. His debut pamphlet *Hearing Ourselves Think* (Smiths Knoll, 2009) was a *Guardian* Book of the Year. A second pamphlet, *Just Help Yourself* (Smiths Knoll), appeared in 2016. *Jelly Baby*, a film-poem, screened at various short film festivals and was published by *Areté*.

PHILIP HANCOCK

City Works Dept.

for Val

from the past to the present

[signature]

5·11·18

CB *editions*

First published in 2018
by CB editions
146 Percy Road London W12 9QL
www.cbeditions.com

Printed in England by T J International, Padstow

ISBN 978-1-909585-27-0

for Michael Laskey

ACKNOWLEDGEMENTS

Acknowledgments are due to the editors of the following: *Areté*, *Magma*, *Nth Position*, *The North*, *Oxford Magazine*, *Oxford Poets 2010* (Carcanet), *Poetry London*, *Poetry Review*, *The Poetry Paper* (Aldeburgh Poetry Festival 2007), *The Rialto*, *Smiths Knoll* and *The Spectator*.

Thanks to Arts Council England for a writer's award which enabled the completion of this manuscript.

Hawthornden International Retreat for Writers for a Fellowship in 2016.

Special thanks to Michael Laskey, Joanna Cutts and David Allison.

What matters to me is the passionate energy of the idea

– Robert Musil

Contents

CITY WORKS DEPT.

To Carry a Ladder

Daft trying to fang hold of it in the middle
or grabbing it wherever suits fit.
Take one end and lift.

Run it up to the sky on its heel.
Get a shoulder under it – take the weight,
and feel for the point of fulcrum.

Allow it to settle on the clavicle,
horizontal, hardly there.
Fist a rung, no sweat:

between parked cars, down entries;
one arm around it, the other swinging.
Beware of washing lines.

New Shoes for the Parade

Naylors – Boyswear on the first floor.
Wax polish lingers from the panelled walls
and oak staircase. I giggle
as the nice lady lifts my foot.
She cups a heel, slides the steel gauge
to my toes: a five.
Her brooch is a silver spider.

Red flowers on the storeroom curtain.
I stare at the man
carrying Clarks boxes, he lumbers
on callipers. The lady rustles
tissue wrapping, thumbs the tips
of my toes. *Just say if they pinch you.*
She asks me to walk.

Mobile Library

Landed.

In the grounds of the single-storey clinic,
the mobile library only stays for one day,
Monday. It always rains.

Overlooked by the quiet iron foundry;
surrounded by white and grey horses,
ranch fencing and lush, wide verges.

It has no window to this world, only a thin door,
but something makes me want to join.

A filthy great fish tank: olive green,
two half-moon wheels and County lettering
in gold leaf. On entry it wheezes.

The librarian has fish eyes behind massive specs
and stacks of scribbled hair, never smiles
or speaks. Only claws the spines and lends.

She is a nylon xylophonist.

Every week is towed away
without sound; leaving a dry space,

a missing final page.

Fenced Off

Moon face with pig eyes,
copper tuft, striped pyjamas,
came shrieking, shaking
the chain-link fence
at the end house, jump-started
our hearts, made us run.

One sticky afternoon,
must have been his dad
sat on the step, sleeves rolled up,
a tattoo, scalp showing
through his grey. The quiet
before the school bus with the ramp.

Toys scattering the yard
always too dear for us:
Captain Scarlet's patrol car
in gold, mighty Tonkas,
a David Brown pedal tractor.
Maybe next Christmas.

Likely he'd be no different from me,
ticking them in the catalogue,
outside Playlands kicking up a fuss.
Lie for ages on his belly
on the wonky concrete flags
making engine noises.

Demolition of the Power Station

Coming back up the A34, counting
the pylons. The cooling towers
where the white clouds are made, always there.
A black-tipped chimney, zigzag ironwork,
slanted conveyors. Squat transformers
fenced in. Flashing NCB lorries,
white-hatted Dinky men.

Dynamite day: crowds stand behind barriers.
Their mouths come open, thick dust
boils up and up, and through the clearing
for the first time what lies beyond:
the backs of houses, light green fields,
horses easing up, a line of poplars.

Now the open curve of the new road,
the billboards for retail and office spaces,
families strolling by lakeside apartments,
but the sky's a blankness, nothing but weather.

Ladsandads

The front tyre scuffs the kerb
when I draw up. Switch off.
Give it a minute.
Sunday morningness.
Tarmac is black gloss
with bastard rain. Bell tower
at Hilltop primary.

Over the embankment
they're still at it, on pitches
unfit for cattle. I sit with them
through an inch-down window.
Those muffled tones, yelled instructions,
building to a cheer – a goal
that dies before the muddy ball
gets lumped back to the spot.

Too small to make the intermediates,
timorous by the time I wasn't.
Could he have made the difference?

Forty years on, the bent railings
I used to slip through
just to get a closer look,
same sludge and clay.

Nothing coming, I don't indicate,
pull away, picking up speed.

The Girl from the Triangle House

for Kerry Davis

A gunshot in a one-horse town
is the clack of the latch
of her garden gate. Starlings flit
to the pylons. Boundary hawthorns stir.
Our trailing feet brake the roundabout.

Lithe and angular with a paprika Afro,
she jigs behind a World Cup football.
Forty keep-ups then shooting-in;
Rigger's drawn the short straw,
paddles in the crater beneath the crossbar,

always fooled by her touch.
The ball gummed to the criss-cross
lacing of her left boot, I'm wrong-
footed by her step-over,
undone by her nutmeg.

Simple passing long after the Evening Sentinels
have been posted and the three blind mice run off
with Giannasi's Ices, until paraffin heat
sweats greenhouse panes and empty buses
flicker between the houses like cine film.

Tonight, the stone I dribble along the pavement
won't escape me. I turn for home,
head full of those orange freckles
coming out like stars, of boots like hers,
Pumas with the white flash.

6 x Concrete Garages

1

'Sad Sweet Dreamer' climbs two places in the charts,
drifts from Chimp-boy's Cooper S, jacked up each Saturday.
Just his legs and the clicks of his ratchet.

2

Turner. Briefcase and glossy black gloves,
eases down his door Monday to Friday, before *Newsround*,
checks the catch is fast, strides off, glances back more than once.

3

Platypus-face got spotted down shaggers lane with Chadwick
of Baskeyfield & Chadwick Builders Ltd. The ticker ticker
of her VW, that stretch she does for the up-and-over.

4

Stacked high with coal. Every evening the scrape
of George's shovel, the Maxi loaded down with sacks.
His lean blonde daughter sometimes calls him in at tea time.

5

Hair in a bun, shiny plum buckled shoes, Mrs Paskin, organist
at the Methodist. At the wheel of her square car she goes
dead slow, her nose almost touches the windscreen.

6

No tyre treads. Dandelions, thistles knee high.
We won't be told again to keep away. Round the back,
give each other leg-ups, but the glass is frosted.

Hillside Foundry

It was a dark blue October afternoon
when the furnace cracked.
Sirens spiralled from the town.
Shouts across our slow street –
It's the foundry!

Its limewashed frontage towered
our jumbled hillside, high windows
hooded by deep eaves. Stepping down
through its braced oak door: darkness,
ringing hammers, stench of casting.

I scrambled upstairs to see
intense orange hurting the sky,
heightening the walls.
Flickering vehicles slammed past
our ribbed-glass porch.

Dad came late from work. Stammered
at the flowing iron lanes,
the warped, ornamental gateway,
the peeled roof and charred blank windows.
His teacup chinked.

Peering along the puddled track
from the comings and goings on Chapel Lane,
I can see its skeleton façade
beyond the chained entrance. Cycle
away, pushing down hard.

The Ledge

I cried myself to sleep when he took them away:
the UFO Shadow tank with flip-over
launcher and red-tipped missiles;
the Merryweather Marquis fire tender
with operating water pump, its real hose.

Out of earshot, he was every swearword
after he confiscated the combat knife
Deano slipped me during history;
the catapult I fired at Johnson's greenhouse –
its square rubber knackered.

Clearing the pantry, I hand them
to my mother from the ledge above the door,
along with the cellophane-bound stack
of Benson & Hedges
the doctor warned him against

and a handful of Everton mints,
gooey in their wrappers. And here's the key
to the bottom drawer of his bedroom chest
beside the instruction manual
for our rusting lawnmower.

Woodruff & Sons

Along the pot-holed track beside the opencast
the recovery truck leaves again, almost six o'clock.
Now's our chance: nip through the corrugated gates.
Foden cabs in a row – ghosts of the A-road –
their doors fused by rust, tyres crazed.
Sports wheels rare as stereos, chrome logos prised off.
Head office is a Luton van where filing cabinets
won't stay shut and Suzie bursts
from last September. Deeper in,
stacked carcasses wait. An engine
fires up. *Fuck*. The flywheel on the crane's high jib
turning. The back of the operator's head,
his shoulders working. We freeze, edge away,
scarper. The telephone rings and rings.

Over 21s

Ritzy's on Friday or Saturday
meant a collar and a proper jacket.
The Dunn & Co tweed dad wore to the office,
he'd be bound to notice not hanging
in the hall. Click open his side
of the wardrobe: fuddy-duddy,
the olive corduroy with leather elbows.
And just imagine being spotted
in that 70s plum with the beige check
and monster lapels. We wanted
to look *Miami Vice* slick: peach shirts,
peppermint kegs, no socks. Have to be
the Weetabix suit jacket he wore
to Cath's wedding, bit long in the sleeves,
but I'd be nodded past the bouncers,
in seconds have it checked in at the cloakroom.
3 a.m. creeping through the house.
How to put it back without him knowing?
Let alone having to explain
why I wouldn't be seen dead in it.

Empty House

The threadbare Axminster lifted without fuss
exposes a pitch-pine deck: staples,
tacks, stubborn gripper rods.

As we wrestled stuffed bin-bags
through the narrow hallway,
the sparkling stud that cost me

slipped from her lobe,
bounced, tinkled, was gone.
Here the floorboards are nailed down solid.

I prod along the gaps with a straightened coat-hanger
while she hovers in her tight cotton blouse
and needle corduroys,

paces the living room, fidgets at the bay window,
thumbs her mobile. *Fuck's sake leave it.*
I didn't like them anyway.

Rented Room

Salvaged from a 50s wardrobe,
the mirror's propped on the radiator.

The ash blonde who made sports cars brake:
Is my left breast really that much smaller?

No shift this weekend, the yawning waiter
scratches his armpit, sniffs his fingers.

The trainee book-keeper, trying out moves
to Donna Summer, ready for the works do.

Every Tuesday Madam unclasps her case,
chains and blindfolds her pharmacist.

The young couple laugh at the mirror
with its bleached football sticker, picked at.

They'll live for now with the thin curtains,
admitting each change in the light.

Half Day

How many times he looks down,
follows that segment of shade
creeping around the main office block,
waits for the windscreens
on the red ash car park to blaze.

With Smythron summoned to head office,
his partition's off their radar:
Geoff's deep in his Sudoku,
Doug's back by the kettle.
He logs off and blows them a kiss.

Foot down on the empty roads,
past the long-closed electrical shop,
that van abandoned in the field.
Window unwound, hairs
alive on his arm.

His boy's in class, his wife's
fielding calls for the doctors
on the other side of town. Straight
to the garden: fixing flagstones
on a semi-dry mix.

Cold grit of sharp sand
between his fingers – one handful
to steady a rocker, tapped into place
with the handle of the hammer,
and another brushed into the gaps.

The spirit level spot on.
It can rain now. Scuffing out his fag,
tea gone cold on the boundary wall,
he takes it all in.
He could almost live here.

The Great Concert Hall

Where skirting boards are skirting boards,
nineteen inches high. Gold balcony rails,
mahogany banisters. Fruit baskets,
picked out in emperor purple and honeysuckle,
top the marble columns, good enough to eat.
The clock tower through the long arched window.
To complete the feature wall: one roll of flock per drop.
Working off a three-stage scaffold, steady hands
guide each length to the plumb, smooth it out,
expel the air. Talk is their years at sea: *that second officer
flattened by a motorbike – middle of the Pacific!*
In the big mirror above the spotless sinks
they slick their white hair, check for paint,
head off, leaving the gallery seats flipped back.
Tuesday it's badminton, Bruno's disco on Friday,
Darby and Joan every Thursday afternoon:
tea, orange squash, biscuits on paper plates.

Apprentice

Access to the rooftops of the indoor market
was via a tiny casement window
in the gods of the adjoining Town Hall.

You'd better have your wits about you up there,
the chargehand warned. *You'll only fall once!*
Whitewashing the skylights: doddle of a job.

Friday, market day in Tunstall. The town's alive
like rainbow sherbet on the tongue. Spacemen
enter the shiny stone bank from their armadillo truck.

Queues outside the chippy and oatcake shop
tilt as a fire engine hustles through
the staggered traffic. Dudsons' kilns

beyond the bus depot. The chargehand
will have filled out our time sheets
and be taking forty winks in the basement.

Beneath the whir of the extractor fans:
the rattle of a shutter door, the rise
and fall of the butcher's spiel, a swirl

of bebop from the record stall. Gorgeous
Trish swallow-dives across her fruit and veg
and Darlo flicks a fag end from the Sneyd Arms steps.

I stand among lions, gargoyles and angels;
watch my good friend John, apprenticed
to the undertaker, waxing the Daimler.

A Drink with the Captain

After lunch, the apprentices egg him on.
Last week it was the Magellan Strait,
that one where the kitten grew and grew,
prowled the deck. *Davy's hat. No Davy.*
Today it's Madagascar: the merchant ship
off course, torpedoes, sharks.
One sweep of his freckled hand:
I knew exactly what to do. Later, he'd sipped
malt matured in sherry casks with the Captain.
Rain pummels our Portakabin.
Through the window, the backs of the estate:
missing tiles, peeling frames, dogs,
still over an hour before we can go.

Pudding, Peas and Gravy

Right you are, son, the gaffer nodded,
after wiping the face of his Casio watch:
Friday's special order for me to down tools early,
to beat the crush, the queue huddled
beneath the chippy's fascia.

No time for checking my reflection
in Naylors' long windows, I hugged
the sweating carton over the zebra crossing,
looked the other way
not to be sussed by Darlo's mob

loitering outside the Sneyd Arms,
snakes inked around their biceps.
And Jack the Cap, the glass collector
with rat's teeth,
always reaching to ruffle my hair.

Nipped along the high street,
the wolf-whistles from the women
with dusty white ankles, off the pot banks,
flushing my face, cooling
in the subway beneath the boulevard.

Blanked by the girl from the solicitor's,
Tupperware box on her lap, nibbling
in the memorial gardens. Up three storeys
to the college annexe, past mining apprentices
kicking the vending machine,

I place his usual, stack a mini-pyramid
of silver and copper pence
he reckons up. Picking apart
the soggy wrapping he sighs, *One day, son,
I'll teach you how to carry gravy.*

Martini Man

Blondes, brunettes, ginger nuts,
I've had 'em all, sunshine. Could be
Janet the cleaner in the library basement,
or that Irish cook with the hips
at the day nursery. A dead cert's
his best mate's wife, Pat.

But in the back of his minivan?
Unsnaring her heel from his bosun's chair,
ruining her tights on a gripper rod.
From the dust sheet, wood slivers
and flecks of paint stick to her arse,
her perfume made nameless by linseed.

He'll lie back thinking of cricket bats
and summer fences, tell her
how it works for kneading old putty:
softening it up, bringing it to life.
Got to look after your hands:
golden rule for any tradesman.

Lessons in Glazing

In a sun without warmth,
late in the year for outside work,
he shows me how
to knead a five-pound keg of putty,
to get to grips with it:

squish it between my fingers,
work it until my aching palms
have made it lump-free, pliable.
A clean knife, vital:
so as not to drag.

Would I ever be as quick:
his deft finger-and-thumbings,
keeping such even pressure.
Off each smoothed, angled
strip, I ease the surplus.

Next morning, my praised work
pitted, gouged-out chunks of it
litter the grass. *Magpies.*
They're after the oil.
All you can do is do it again.

Margarine

works a treat, mum had said.
The girls start on his specs,
take it in turns,
their tentative fingers
don't know how much
is too much pressure
till he shifts in the armchair.
Trying not to catch each other's eye,
they swallow the giggles.
Move on to his nose
and the flecks of paint
on his cheeks, his chin –
until they see him at last,
can't laugh any more:
their dad, his saggy skin,
his breath like the air
from a beach ball
collapsing and collapsing.

A Year On

but her tears again
as I turf the rose beds,
trade his long-winged Ford
for a car she can park.
Forty-four's no age.

The wardrobe gapes his side
since I bagged his stuff
for Barnardo's. And now some of hers:
everyday skirts, that anorak
off the catalogue.

I point out smart heels in Ravel,
catch her giggle in the window.
Benetton colours jazz her up:
she's still got the figure,
sod the neighbours.

She drapes them over the bed,
frets about what goes best
with what, holds them up
against herself in the mirror:
Not like they were in the shop.

Hadge's Encyclopedia

All summer he lugged it round,
twisting his jumper to hide the elbows.
Some afternoons he'd let us see:
cloth-bound, crimson, gilt-edged.
Only the pictures,
his black nails flipping the pages:
brontosauruses in a misted lake,
the deep-sea diver's bronze helmet,
fish with needle teeth, mansion-sized
quarry machines, biplanes.
Some pages he'd score with biro,
others tear out. Weeks later,
behind the green garages
where the wind had given it up,
we found one: a smart family
outside their new home, a hole
where the mum's face had been,
saloon car on the drive, a lawn.

Mr Gaunt's Class

We step back as they pass
after the morning bell: boy girl, boy girl,
hand in hand along the infants' corridor.

Their shoes gleam like new cars; clothes
the colours of seaside homes. Wide-eyed –
we're strange men, the pong of our paint.

Keep to one side. They do as the navy pinstripe
commands. He knows best, and skips
over our chevron barrier tape

beyond the fluorescent cones;
drills them into assembly. The dado
scuffed by his hip will have to be repainted.

Head down for prayers, he'll clock it, pale
pink that white spirit won't shift.
The Lord's my Shepherd. We hum along.

Perks

In the end you're relieving his headache,
freeing up space in the storeroom:
five-litre bottles of PVA shunted back further
from the caretaker's mind. He won't clock
two missing among kegs of floor sealant,
tins of crusted polish.

A week or two, no hurry.
Pick your time. Maybe best at 4:30
when you know he'll be flanked by his assistant,
bossing his cleaners around the classroom block.
Get the wife to pick you up
by the windowless boiler house.

Come in handy one day, you always said:
EXIT lights, a box of test tubes,
a dinner service stamped 'Chaney House',
that hospital porter's red trolley.

Hours in Hand

No one would give them a second glance:
backsides of out-house doors untouched,
guttering and fascia boards skimped,
upstairs rear windows painted shut.
Flat out around the blocks of houses
to bank the hours, ensure our bonuses
should the weather change. And if it doesn't,
what to do with all that time? Take turns
to slip off early, fire-proof excuses
should he show up at five to five.
Years of studying how best to avoid
working. Back home we piddle about
in our sheds or garages; thumb the remote,
slump in front of *Ivor the Engine*.

Rained Off

Any straightened two-foot length
of three-quarter-inch copper pipe,
bent tight at one end. Silver foil
tamped down the barrel with a garden cane.
Sulphur next, finger-nailed off the heads
of half a household box of matches. More silver foil.
Ball bearings or smooth pebbles, five or six.
We poked the business end through the air hole
of a common brick, to steady its aim
at the door of our mess, took cover
beneath the Formica-topped tables
as the blowtorch reddened the metal.

Sheer luck no one came breezing in.

Girder Bashers

Cut-throat targets, but top bonus
plus overtime. Stanway's arm first up,
JT, Salty, two others, twelve's the gang.
Double time from 6 a.m. tramping
the hard shoulder of the A500,
coning off the approach to City flyover.
Beneath it we nimble on a 10 x 10-foot tower
braced to the flat-bed Iveco truck,
follow up the pneumatic needle-gun
with red-oxide primer on the RSJs,
yell down to the driver to shift us over.
All day east–west traffic thunders
just above our heads. Below,
rocking our rig, the whop of coaches,
haulage, flashing reps. Sometimes we ease up,
watch them as far as the floodlights
at the Victoria Ground, heading for the M6,
miles to go. And so have we: another coat
before rush hour. Sweating in boiler-suits
we crouch and stretch, over-reach,
bang it on, can't hear ourselves think.

The Quiet Joiner

He came to us at the halfway house –
snipped moustache, overalls spotless
as his politely-parked Volkswagen –
to hang fifteen sapele fire doors
in three days.

We bet on his chances:
four flights of narrow stairs,
suspended ceilings, new lino,
how not to mash his fingertips
in the gunshot closers.

After circling his car, lunch:
brown bread sandwiches, a tomato,
pepper tapped from a pill bottle,
proper time taken
over each closed mouthful.

The last day glossing up:
Fucking flies, we're stripped
to the waist, full blast
Radio 1, coming in
on the chorus.

Him just stood there,
returning the steel rule
to his breast pocket:
All done.
The only time we heard him speak.

Knowing One's Place

After the miles behind,
the years catching up,
I'm on that beach with Meursault,
the sun of Algiers unforgiving,

turning another page
of this browning paperback
I'd covered with Stoke City's
'79 season first team pull-out.

In the Portakabin, the chat
tails off. *Summat someone lent me*, I say,
spitting bits of salmon paste.
Crooksey. Alan Dodd. Great side that.

The Summer Temp

Big as Canada –
where he'd worked the railroads –
Jesus hair and beard,
gum-soled shoes and jumbo cords,
hands the size of stranglers
in black and white films, perfect
for dealing with caretakers
and roofing. He kept on
how everything was bigger over there:
cranes, hinges, bathrooms.
We smirked at his buckskin toolbag,
his chisels as chisels should be.
One day I'll get out of Stoke,
I told him, do something different.
I had dreams once, kiddo.

Double Take

at his gait, that slight lean to the left,
the lightness of those ballroom feet,
no tie.

In Lewis's, the sales.
You pray he's not seen you,
riffle the clothes rail.

On the job, his voice down the corridor
and we snap back to work,
trying to act natural.

He's there with the muzak
right beside you, just another man.
This is my good lady, son.

Dress Sense

Why is it when you step into a caff
flash in your scarf, you wish you could hide
from the gang of scaffolders?
Not the hoodies and tattoos, but those
that eye you. Where does it come from,
your irritation at how quick they'll be done,
swaggering in grey sweatpants,
their wages always bigged up?
Those with teeth have brilliant teeth.

When you stop to think of what they do:
heights and levels sussed at a glance,
no hands at forty feet in the rain,
working for each other, you can let go
their slinging of doubles and pigs' ears,
hollering for 12s and 21s, boards slammed,
Reebok feet on the dashboard of their cab.
And if you slope in in your splattered overalls,
don't you face them square on: *All right, fellas?*

New Development

Each time I returned,
it got smaller – pallets of bricks,
scaffolding, barge boards and fences –

that field of clumps and tufts,
nothing much. Not bad for a kickabout,
but the business was the pond.

Mountford strode with that face on,
an authority
on all matters freshwater.

Kids in wellies dipped stick nets,
orange and green, skimmed jam jars
for spawn and taddies.

The hard-liners trampled
grass and mud, reeds and rushes,
waded in up to their Y-fronts.

But what really counted
only levered up with luck
in net-loads of weed and sludge:

the great crested newt –
held in my palm, plopped back –
that's put a stop to the building.

Top Storey

Flash of arse, slammed door
as I appear. Froth of knickers
on the bed when I slide the lower sash up.
Not that anybody would believe it,
but – four rungs from the top of a ladder
fully extended, footed by a wheelie bin,
a casual wedge against death –
what I want is windows:

windows that slide sweetly, overlap
enough for painting the middle rail,
for the gloss to flow just right
and cut in sharp to the edge,
everything reachable, no snags,
not her coming back from the shower.

French Windows

He never seems to go out.
And now he's right behind me.

Have you missed a bit there?
My wrist stiffens.

The house phone takes him away,
lets me get back to what I do

without thinking.
A steady hand, almost perfect.

Tomorrow's World

It'll never catch on,
this gismo, zapper or thingamajig
on the arm of the best chair.

Sleek plastic slab: moulded to suit
the standard hand; infrared
channelled through its diode.

But how much tug-o'-warring, bouncing
off floors, or whacking over skulls
can it endure? *Get tha' off. Giz it.*

Not foreseen by those ergonomic
lab coats, intent on the next model.
Four to the average home.

Quarter Glass

Obtuse triangle of light
separate from the door windows,
front mainly. Pivotable:
rush of cooling air let in
by finger and thumb. Easy to work.

But now always sealed
in rubber frames.
Nothing of note until,
after a shower has passed,
light falls on the dashboard dust.

Loft

Where the membrane's come away
from the rafters: nicks of light,
and whatever else gets under the tiles.

Astray from their nest in the eaves,
wasps wheel and crawl, a mower
gives up, a shudder of wind brings

children making the sounds of children.
The scratch of claws overhead,
wings whir away. Baked heat.

A done sum of beams and joists.
The block of the water tank
presses steadily on.

Cases with rusted catches, boxfuls
of albums of who and where's that,
and you now and then poking through,

trying to get your head around it.

Hall

No one stays in the hall.
Feeder of the main rooms,
it misses little.

If the kitchen's the heart
of the home,
the hall's its ears.

The opening and closing of doors
make news of what's going on
clear, more or less.

Excitement at a delivery,
a pause for dark shapes in the glass,
now the bell insists no one's in.

It waits on the green telephone,
a bicycle leaning on the radiator,
talk of adding a storm porch.

Geometry

That afternoon it was Geometry
but at the classroom door, mum.
Where the houses gave way to Harding's fields,
she told me: *Granddad . . . in his sleep.*
Crosswinds muffled her words.
Empty driveways along Bullocks House Road,
the petrol pump attendant's feet – his face
behind a magazine. In the lounge
Aunt Lily slurped tea from a saucer.
Nana's red eyes, ruddy cheeks; dad didn't speak.
The paperboy nipped along the terrace
opposite, buses got fuller, tail-lights came on.
In the blackening glass I saw us all in another room.

Inside Job

Just help yourself to anything.
She's away into the morning drizzle.
No more than five minutes
before you switch *Woman's Hour*
to CD to OFF; settle instead
for that leaking gutter outside,
the tick of rainwater on sycamore leaves,
the grandmother clock in the hall.
Your work in her bedroom as good as done,
only the mahogany bookcase to put back.
Her books: Roald Dahl with a purple cover,
Henry Miller, the big Americans. Photos slip
from *Delta of Venus*: a grinning beard –
the ex? – and ones of her: retro pubes,
body white as a fridge, on all fours.
Nothing on top of the wardrobe. Lace
and lace and lace springs from her dresser.
Swivel open the bedside cabinet: condoms,
a wad of letters. Downstairs a click,
metal on metal, takes your breath.

The Family Business

Halide-lit, it draws me in.
Almost homely: Welsh dresser
undressed of its china. Set for four,
the dining table, white candles.
On either side of the polished aisles
plenty more: three-piece suites,
nest of tables, mirrors I shy
away from, pictures of mountains,
a pottery leopard filling a corner.
Same time all day, the shop
goes back much further.
I try an easy chair, imagine
myself really sitting in it.
Wonder how best to slip out
past the assistant, into the open.

Caravans

They crowd Smithsons storage ground
off the Liverpool Road. Will be towed out
by a rust-scabbed tractor, fussed over
on grass-verged avenues, Turtle-waxed.
A long weekend on the outskirts of a coastal town
or that once-yearly fortnight, Potters' shutdown.

Beds spring from veneered panelling,
a cottage teapot on a shelf,
horse brasses and framed photos.
From the bow window, high kites
in the afternoon, a Ferris wheel pauses.

Too soon they're ball-and-hitched again,
following empty. Tailgated by HGVs,
they snake in the crosswind.
As the motorway approaches the viaduct
the driver demands hush, clenches the wheel.

Running on Red

You still have to think
which side's the fuel cap.
Beneath the canopy
you watch digits flicker
pounds for litres, quick as a blink.
Queue at the kiosk, a Snickers, why not,
punch in your pin. Hurry
to be back in the warmth
of your miles, the pre-set radio.
You pull away across the forecourt,
no more than a glance
at the cars at the pumps
or the others after water or air.

Giannasi

Invisible jingle somewhere
between five and six.
Notes you know by heart but where?
Rousing a crescent or cul-de-sac,
coming this way.
How long will it wait
for you at the corner?
How many years?